Heavenly Realm Publishing
Houston, Texas

Emphasis within Scripture quotations is the author's own. Please note that Stephanie Franklin capitalizes all pronouns in Scripture that refer to God. The name "satan" and related references are not capitalized intentionally.

This book is protected by the copyright laws of the United States. This book may not be copied or reprinted for commercial gain or profit. No part of this book may be reproduced, stored in a retrieval system, or transmitted by any means, electronic, mechanical, photocopying, recording, or otherwise, without written permission from the author or publisher.

Copyright © 2014 by, Stephanie Franklin, The Power of Healing: *A Biblical Guide on How to be Healed Spiritually, Mentally, Physically, and Emotionally and Maintain Your Healing*. All rights reserved.

Published by, Heavenly Realm Publishing
PO Box 682532
Houston, TX 77268
1-866-216-0696

Visit our Website at: www.heavenlyrealmpublishing.com

Printed in the United States of America

ISBN—13- 978-1-937911-75-1
ISBN—10- 1937911751

Library of Congress Control Number—2014910697
Stephanie Franklin
The Power of Healing: *A Biblical Guide on How to be Healed Spiritually, Mentally, Physically, and Emotionally and Maintain Your Healing* / Stephanie Franklin

Body, Mind, & Spirit: Healing-Prayer & Spiritual—United States. 2. Body, Mind, & Spirit: Healing- General—United States. 3. Religion: Biblical Studies- General—United States.

This book is printed on acid free paper.

Unless otherwise indicated, all scriptures quotations in this book are from the King James Version of the Holy Bible, and NIV version.

Stephanie Franklin
Stephanie Franklin Ministries
www.stephaniefranklinministries.org
info@stephaniefranklinministries.org

The POWER of Healing

A Biblical Guide on How to be Healed Spiritually, Mentally, Physically, and Emotionally and Maintain Your Healing.

Stephanie Franklin

Heavenly Realm Publishing
Houston, Texas

Table of Contents

INTRODUCTION   **13**

CHAPTER ONE:
Help from the Healer:
He is Almighty and He's Come to Heal   **21**

CHAPTER TWO:
Healing in the Mind:
The Mind of Christ is the Only Way   **27**

CHAPTER THREE:
Healing in Faith:
You Must Believe and Not Waiver   **33**

CHAPTER FOUR:
30 for 30:
Healing Through the Word of God   **37**

CHAPTER FIVE:
Healing in the Body:
Steps and Scripture to Ensure Healing   **55**

CHAPTER SIX:
Healing in Your Praise:
The Praise Break   **73**

CHAPTER SEVEN:
Power to Maintain Your Healing:
Remind God of His Word Daily   **79**

CONCLUSION   ***83***
INDEX   ***85***
BIBLICAL INDEX SOURCES FROM EACH CHAPTER   ***86***
ADDITIONAL HEALING SCRIPTURES   ***87***

BOOKS BY STEPHANIE

FICTION NOVELS:
1. When Ramona Got Her Groove Back from God
2. My Song of Solomon
3. My Song of Solomon *Prayer Journal*
4. God Loves Thugs Too!

MOTIVATIONAL BOOK:
5. *The Locker Room Experience: For the Struggling Athlete & Coach, & Tips on How to Get Recruited in Sports*

MINISTRY BOOKS & WORKBOOK:
6. Position Your Faith for Great Success
7. Position Your Faith for Great Success *Workbook*
8. The Purpose Chaser: *For Children Ages 5 to 12*
9. Church Hurt: *How to Heal & Overcome It*
10. *The Power of Healing*
11. *The Power of the Holy Spirit*
12. *Do it On Purpose*

The POWER of Healing

Jesus died so that you and the whole nation could live.

John 11:50

INTRODUCTION

In this day and time there are so many events that have occurred that have made Christian Believers wonder if God's healing and miracles still exists. Some wonder if they ever existed. I have learned that words from man can be wrong and misconstrued; however, the Words of the Holy Bible will always stand for forever. If there are ever any questions or wonders, the Holy Bible is always the answer. The old saying still stands strong, "Just go to the Word." I'm in agreement, we should all just go to the Word (Bible).

If there are ever any questions as to whether or not God's healing and miracles are real, it is proven through our Lord and Savior Jesus Christ Who made it a priority to show these imperative actions to help the people to believe. Miracles of healing were done so that the people would not stay stagnant to unbelief, but would turn to the Lord through faith and belief. He demonstrated this powerful effort in His days here on earth as spoken in the books of Matthew, Mark, Luke, and John; as they all share their rendition of His genealogy, kingdom assignment, ministry, purpose, and truth. Most of all, they all prove His sacrifice of love for us all as He suffered and died on the cross, and later resurrected so that we can have eternal life.

He healed the sick and raised the dead on numerous occasions. No one can deny that these actions were true, because they were. Just as miracles were true then, they still are today. The Bible says, He's the same yesterday, today, and forever more (Hebrews 13:8). His Word stands and endures forever, it never changes (1 Peter 1:25). So, since He did it then, He is still doing it today. There are many testimonies who will stand in agreement with me. Yours may be one of them. Well, with that said, He can do it for you and/or for someone you know who is suffering with an unbearable illness. He is a miracle worker. He is a doctor in the sick room. He is a lawyer in the courtroom. He is a friend when you need Him. He is everything. *The Power of Healing* is for you if you want it.

Jesus not only worked miracles, healed the sick, and raised the dead, but He used his people—disciples and people of God to do the same. Just to name a few, he used Paul, a mighty man of God who was converted from an unbeliever and once persecuted the Christian Believers. Jesus used many as it is proven in the book of Acts. Jesus used his people and things in order to help the people to believe. For example, in Acts 19:11-20, Jesus used clothing that had touched Paul's skin to heal the sick as he used handkerchiefs, aprons, towels, etc. and placed them on the sick people. As a result, diseases, sicknesses, and evil spirits went out of the people. God will use anything, He can anoint anything, and

Introduction

anyone to do the assigned work that He is trying to do at that moment. His glory is at stake. Therefore, He will do anything to make that happen. Just as he used the clothing that touched Paul's skin, He was responsible to heal the people for His glory. It was not the clothing that did it, it was the Holy Spirit and the powerful anointing that healed the people. So, just as God healed the people, He can also heal you through His Word. In this case, Paul's assignment was to spread the gospel and heal (through God) the people any way possible. So, if your pastor, church, or ministry, have ever used anointed prayer clothes and have passed them out to the congregation of people, <u>only if God leads you to</u>, I encourage you to take one and do just as the man or woman of God tells you. It will work. If God leads you to read this book and to do the 30 for 30 day challenge in chapter four, do it, there is an anointing on that, it will only work with your faith and if you believe.

During my journey in ministry, traveling from place to place praying for the sick, it never dawned on me to write a book on healing until the Lord quickened me to do so. All of these years of praying and have experienced seeing the sick healed in Jesus Name, watched miracles happen right before my eyes, it never dawned on me to write a book on healing and share some of my experiences as God used my gift to heal. I have witnessed the power of God performed right before my eyes. One I will share.

Stephanie Franklin

There was a time when a man I knew, I will not share his name, complained about having an excruciating pain in his mid-back area. The man was persistent in telling me about his pain every time I seen him, which was on a daily basis. I knew God was using his persistence. So, I finally told him that God has given me a gift to heal and that I could pray and believe God that the pain would leave his back, and he would be healed. He quickly agreed and said he believe that it will. Before praying, I placed my hand on his mid-back, and noticed that there was a huge bulge of a knot about the size of a fist. I immediately knew it was something more serious than just muscle fatigue. As I laid hands on his back (prayerfully placed my hand on his mid-back) and began to pray by commanding the knot to be removed, the huge knot immediately began to subside until I could no longer feel it. I could feel that it had removed completely. He began to move back a little, trying not to fall back due to the release of the power of healing from that knot, but did not. I knew he was healed and he did too. I asked him how he felt as he sighed and said he felt good. I then asked him was the pain gone, and he could not wait to say the pain was gone. From that day forward, he has not ever complained about having back pains again. Praise God! That is how the power of God comes. My belief in God. My faith in God. His belief in God. His faith in God. Our faith connection of agreement (coming together and believing in

Introduction

faith), and as a result, the manifested miracle of healing was performed.

Just as miracles of healing have happened right before my eyes, there were times when I prayed and nothing happened. I could not understand because I knew I was in faith for the person(s), and I knew that when God used me to pray and lay hands on the sick, they recovered. However, this time it was different, it did not happen. I became discouraged and sought the Lord for an answer. He spoke to me and told me that it was because they did not believe or they were too afraid. In order for instant healing to manifest, faith must first be ignited. You cannot doubt or be afraid. You cannot lean or put everything on the pastor, minister, reverend, prayer warrior, or the person praying for you. It must first come through your faith.

There have been cases where I have prayed and the person who was in need of prayer believed but did not see their manifestation of healing right away, so they gave up. Just because you do not see your manifestation right away does not mean that giving up is an option. There are times it is a process according to your faith. The key here is to make sure that you are constantly in faith during the process so that the manifestation will come forth as quick as possible. In the Word of God, it says that faith the size of a mustard seed can move mountains (Matthew 17:20). Mountains are huge and a mustard seed is very small. You only have to use this same small faith to believe without wavering in order to see your instant miracle healing come to past in a huge way.

> *"And Jesus said unto them, Because of your unbelief: for verily I say unto you, If ye have faith as a grain of mustard seed, ye shall say unto this mountain, Remove hence to yonder place; and it shall remove; and <u>nothing shall be impossible</u> unto you."*
>
> **Matthew 17:20**

No one understands the power of healing until you have become very ill and have had to turn to the Lord for help. It is an amazing feeling to be healed by God; in fact, there is no other feeling or touch that can compare. Those who were sick in the book of Matthew experienced the same thing through the healing power of Jesus Christ's ministry, as He prayed for them and they recovered. You may ask, "how in the world can I believe to be healed?" I will answer, believe, and imagine by faith that you are healed. Imagine that the sickness you are encountering is gone—disappeared as you trust God.

There was a time I had a tumor in my uterus the size of a softball. I went to get an annual checkup and the doctor stated that the tumor was large and gave me some options. I told the doctor that I did not want them to take my uterus and that I

Introduction

would pray about it. I left praying. I reminded God of His Word. I confessed my healing. I believed that I was healed and not sick. I trusted God. God quickly gave me my answer. As I have prayed for many, the Lord revealed to me to pray and to lay hands on myself, and so I did. As I laid my hands on my lower stomach area, prayed God's Word loudly, and commanded that the tumor leave, I could miraculously feel the tumor disappear instantly and my stomach went down right before my eyes. This happened because I believed that the tumor was not there and that I was already healed. I cannot say that at first my faith was not tested, and some fear did come when I first heard the doctor's answer. However, I had to quickly get myself together and trust God. So, I reminded God of His Word and that He did not promise me that tumor. God is our mighty power and He is our Strong Tower, and He came to heal us as we exemplify our faith to believe for instant healing, it must come forth and it did for me. It can happen for you too.

God is no respect of persons. He has poured out the same measure of healing to you as He has across the globe to those who believe. He has given all of us the power to do anything—to be healed, to acquire wealth, to get out of debt, to share the gospel, to be kind to one another, to wake up in the morning in our right mind, to go to work, and so on. The power belongs to us. It is freely given to us to use it as we please. Thank God, we do not have to pay for healing. It is free. So why not use it when it is needed?

The power in which healing obtains has no comparisons. You know when you have been healed as the Holy Spirit and the power of God lets you know. There is no other spirit and power that can compare. In fact, they're not even in the running. You have to be confident in this power of healing that God has given to you to use when it is needed. All God requires is that you <u>believe</u>. Look below at the greatness of God's Power in His Word.

> *"And what is the exceeding greatness of his <u>power</u> to us-ward who <u>believe,</u> according to the working of his mighty power."*
>
> **Ephesians 1:19**

> *"Now unto him that is able to do exceeding abundantly above all that we ask or think, according to the <u>power</u> that worketh in us,"*
>
> **Ephesians 3:20**

1

Help from the *Healer*

He is Almighty and He's Come to Heal

Many times we look to people, things, our jobs, family, and friends for help when really the help is right in front of us. God is your Helper. It is all in His Word how He awaits to help you. However, most Christian Believers do not believe that God can really help them or that He can come right away like they need Him too. I have heard this phrase, "God is too slow, I need help right now!" People often laugh at that phrase but it is really not one to take lightly because it hinders your immediate blessing, due to your lack of knowledge to know what the Word of God says about God coming to give you what you need at that hour.

> *"For the Holy Ghost shall teach you in the same hour what ye ought to say."*
>
> **Luke 12:12**

God is our Helper and He is ready to reveal His mighty power to you only if you believe. You can always count on Him. He is your help in time of distress, need, crazy days that might have upset you and don't seem to go right, and/or relationship conflicts you may be encountering. Sometimes it's just little things like, personality and choice disagreements. These constitute mental and emotional battles. You may be in a battle with someone who is always picking at you, picking with your comments or every word you say and you need help from the Lord. It is not always sickness in our bodies, or our delinquent finances, or even something so great and mighty. It is the little foxes. Most times these little foxes is what destroys your health—body, relationships, not wanting anyone to see you in the position you are in, jobs, children, peace, ability to rest at night, your desire to worship God, your quiet time with God—praying and concentration and reading your Bible, and ability to think. Your mind is so cluttered that it is impossible to know where you are at times, along with stress build up that comes to bring sickness and disease. All of these things can be avoided if you go to the Helper, Who is Jesus Christ Who died for the very issue you are having just to give you the victory over that very situation. You have to know that your issue, dilemma, or sickness is already conquered, healed, and destroyed. Again, Jesus died for that very thing. I realize this may sound deep to you. But, it is what it is. It is the truth that can only set you free. Words are irrelevant. They fade away without meat to make a difference or to bring change. But, the Word of the Lord our God will <u>never</u> fade away. It brings change immediately. It brings change instantly.

I can recall a time when I was feeling down and all I had was the Word of God to run to for peace. Right before I opened the Bible, I said a desperate prayer for help in the mist of my distress, and that prayer must have changed my life. Immediately after the prayer, I opened the Bible and went right to what I needed. My miracle was right in front of me. The words on that page came together. They fit what I was going through. They were the right words I needed to hear to give me the right answer to my problems. However, the difference between reading the words in the Bible at that very moment, than the words in any other book was, as I began to read, it brought healing to my soul. Worldly books do not do that, they bring pleasure and lies. I immediately began to feel better. I had a new perspective on my problems. Although the problems I was facing were still there and still needed to be changed, the Word of God gave me a whole new determination and mindset about the situation and how to change them. Meaning, I changed how negative I was speaking, thinking, and feeling against my situation and began to look at them already victorious.

> *"But those things which proceed out of the mouth come from the heart; and they defile the man."*
>
> **Matthew 15:18**

I changed the way I was trying to handle my problems. I was trying to handle them on my own, with my own knowledge and strength, knowing it is not through our own knowledge and strength, it is through God, Who is our Healer and Helper. He changed my mindset to know that He will take care of it and will give me the strength to get through it and to see His salvation and victory. As I began to change the way I thought, my problems changed to victory. I no longer had to face the problems I was going through alone. God gave me the victory and He can do this same thing for you. I encourage you today not to be weary in well doing, for in due season you will reap if you faint not (Galatians

6:9). Do not give up. God has a plan to help you and to give you an expected end (Jeremiah 29:11).

Here are four points on how to receive victory as you trust help from the Healer:

Scripture Focus: Proverbs 3:5-6
1. Take yourself out of the way and allow God to come in and be the center of attention and decisions you make.
2. Go to his Word (the Bible) and see what He has to say about your situation and decisions you should make.
3. Change the way you think (from negative thoughts, words, and ways to positive faith (thoughts, words, and ways that He's already done it).
4. Stand, wait, and keep quiet until God moves. And, I rest assure you He will.

You must know the power God has given to you within. Many of us do not realize the power that we already possess within. This **Power that God has given to us allows us to be able to do anything**, and this power lives within us that is waiting to come out.

but what God has in mind for you is another. What He has in mind is always best. Do not be like the people who just dropped him off with no faith to believe for what the lame man really needed (healing), be like Peter and John and have the faith to believe for you and/or someone else's healing, rather than put material things first. As a result, when you put your faith on healing, material needs after that will <u>not</u> be an issue.

It takes faith for everything. It takes faith to pick up a glass and fill it with water. It takes faith to wake up in the morning, wash your face, brush your teeth, put on your clothes, eat breakfast, and go to work. You cannot be healed without faith. It takes faith to be healed. You may ask, "how do I have faith?" I will answer, just believe that you are already healed, and your healing will manifest before you know it.

> *(1) "Now faith is the substance of things hoped for and the evidence of things not seen."*
>
> *(6) "But <u>without faith</u> it is <u>impossible</u> to please him: for he that cometh to God <u>must believe</u> that he is, and that he is a rewarder of them that diligently seek him."*
>
> **Hebrews 11:1, 6**

2

Healing in the

Mind

The Mind of Christ is the Only Way

The mind is one of the most needed things a human being can have. If the mind goes, the entire body will shut down and go into another mode that is not the will of God. It will make that or those persons operate unstable, dysfunctional, illiterate, and even in a way that would bring discomfort to others around them.

God has provided through His Word the power to keep the mind from shutting down and going in this direction. He wants our minds to be just like His.

The Word of God says:

> *"Let this mind be in you, which is also in Christ Jesus:"*
>
> **Philippians 2:5**

It is God's desire that our minds stay focused on Him and think like Him at all times. Now, please do not take this religiously. What I mean when I say to keep your mind on Him and to think like Him, is to keep your mind on positive things, on right things, on good things, on faith working things, on hopeful things, on things that will bring you happiness on the inside as well as those around you.

> *"...he was wounded for our transgressions, he was bruised for our iniquities: the chastisement of our peace was upon him; and with his strips we are <u>healed</u>."*
>
> **Isaiah 53:5**

We are over taken by daily problems in which come to sidetrack us and get us off focus—off where God is trying to take us; and what He is trying to do with us, through us, and for us. Your belief should <u>not</u> depend on what kind of bad day you had on that day, it should <u>not</u> depend on whether or not there was horrible traffic on your way home from work, it should depend on what the Word of God says about being content in whatever situation or state you are in, be content (Philippians 4:11).

Peter and John were persecuted, as some leaders doubted that Jesus healed the cripple man through Peter and John in Acts chapter 4. They could not believe that it was Jesus, seeing He was not there physically. It is easy to believe in something that you can see, but what more awesome to believe in something that you cannot see. Jesus has left us His precious Holy Spirit to dwell within us, to know that He is always with us and will never leave us (John 14:18, 8-18). Now this should give you comfort to know that Jesus is with you and because He is with you, you're content no matter what you go through; and already healed. I believe that cripple man was healed before the actual physical manifestation came through Peter and John. All he had to do was to believe. All he had to do was to have faith that the power of Jesus Christ could heal him and manifest it. Once he did, healing met him (Peter and John through Jesus) and he was healed. You have to do the same thing. Although you cannot see Jesus in the flesh; and at times you may not feel Him (the Holy Spirit) there with you (in Spirit), and you may not get visitors from the church or family and friends, but you have to believe and be confident in what the Word of God says about your healing.

Stephanie Franklin

United In the Mind

Christian Believers, prayer warriors, and the community of Believers must come together and pray that miracles happen all over the world (In our churches, homes, communities, on our jobs, in our finances, in our families, for our children and their children, if any, for our schools, for our country and other countries, for homeless shelters, for any kind of shelter, and for all of the non-profit organizations helping others, etc.) (Acts 4:24-31). All the believers prayed to God with one purpose.

When the Body of Believers are <u>one</u> in the <u>mind</u> as they all come together, miracles happen immediately. It happened for the Believers, Apostles, and Peter and John. After they had all finished praying, the Bible says they were all filled with the Holy Spirit and the entire room shook with God's power and presence. It also says, they were <u>united</u> in their <u>thinking</u> (mind) and in what they wanted (Acts 4:32). The key to the underlined words here is, "they were *united*, and *thinking* (mind)." You may have to find a prayer partner or covenant partner to team up with you, and come together to believe God for your help and healing. When two or more people are standing agreeing on the same thing, God promises to be in the mist of your prayer and situation. He moves faster when there is more agreeing on the same thing (Matthew 18:16). Not that He will not move with just your prayer, but He moves quicker when there are more praying and agreeing together on the same thing in faith. God desires that the people of God work together, pray together, and are united in unity and in faith.

> *"But if he will not hear thee, then take with thee one or two more, that in the mouth of two or three witnesses every word may be established."*
>
> **Matthew 18:16**

3

Healing in

Faith

You Must Believe and Not Waiver

Money cannot buy you healing. Only Faith can get you healing. The power of faith to believe can only bring healing immediately. Doubting with your mind, heart, and mouth brings you nothing. Do not allow the enemy to make you think positive thoughts one minute, and the next you're thinking thoughts of doubt, and even unbelief. God would rather you be hot or cold, and not lukewarm (Revelation 3:16).

> *(15) "I know thy works, that thou art neither cold or hot:*
> *I would thou wert cold or hot."*
> *(16) "So then because thou art lukewarm,*
> *and neither cold or hot,*
> *I will spew thee out of my mouth."*
>
> Revelation 3:15-16

Many times people wonder why their healing does not come right away. This simply happens due to unbelief, doubting, distraction, and blind leading. Distraction comes when you have a deep desire to go to a church service that you feel will help you to get healed from a problem you are facing, and someone close to you comes along before you leave and speaks against your desire. As a result, you follow the distraction that came as an assignment from the devil to deter you from receiving your healing, and you do not go. Please do not get me wrong, it was not that close person or person who spoke against your possible blessing, it was the devil using them because he knew you would listen to them; and he could use them to stop you from your long awaited healing. This is why it is very important to follow what you know God is leading you to do, stay in faith believing like you know to do, and keep your mouth shut on your way there. You can never go wrong following what God leads you to do. The devil is cunning and he will try to use anyone he can to stop the plan of God. Impossible if you obey. It is always better to obey God than man (Acts 5:29).

Blind leading comes as a setback. It comes to steal the will of God from helping you, completely. Let's look at the lame man in Acts chapter 3. Everyday he was carried and dropped off at the gate of the temple, which was called, "Beautiful." The Bible does not say that they carried him there in hopes to be healed. They just dropped him off. If you look here, this was blind leading. They carried and dropped him there only to believe that maybe he could get alms (money) and maybe, just maybe someone would help him. However, God sent Peter and John with the truth. Their words were, *"Silver and gold have I none, but such as I have give I thee."* It was the Spirit of faith and the power of truth that brought Peter and John there at the right moment and at the right time of day. It was his day of breakthrough. It was his faith and chance to be healed, which had nothing to do with him begging for money. He took it and immediately he began to walk. What I love about this passage of scripture is the fact that God met him where he was, although he had something else on this agenda. As he received his healing, the Bible says that he went into the temple ANYWAY and praised and leaped and praised God. The temple is where he should have gone in the first place instead of looking to money for his answer. Money cannot buy you healing, only faith can. What you have in mind is one thing, but what God has in mind for you is another. What He has in mind is always best. Do not be like the people who just dropped him off with no faith to believe for what the lame man really needed (healing), be like Peter and John and have the faith to believe for you and/or someone else's healing, rather than put material things first. As a result, when you put your faith on healing, material needs after that will <u>not</u> be an issue.

It takes faith for everything. It takes faith to pick up a glass and fill it with water. It takes faith to wake up in the morning, wash your face, brush your teeth, put on your clothes, eat breakfast, and go to work. You cannot be healed without faith. It takes faith to be healed. You may ask, "how do I have faith?" I will answer, just believe that you are already healed, and your healing will manifest before you know it.

(1) "Now faith is the substance of things hoped for and the evidence of things not seen."

(6) "But <u>without faith</u> it is <u>impossible</u> to please him: for he that cometh to God <u>must believe</u> that he is, and that he is a rewarder of them that diligently seek him."

Hebrews 11:1, 6

4

30 for 30

Healing Through the Word of God

REMEMBER TO DO YOUR 30 MINUTE STUDY ON EACH OF THE HEALING SCRIPTURES DAILY. THEY ARE LOCATED ON THE CHART IN THIS CHAPTER.

Many people go to bookstores or order books online, and some even spend their last. I say that to say, the Bible is the last thing they will spend their time needing or reading until something detrimental happens, or a major life ending sickness arise. Healing comes through the Word of God (the Bible). Jesus healed through His Word and by His faith to believe that anybody would be healed if they believed. Although books are good to encourage and help toward your healing, the Bible is the best book to receive healing right away.

God has given me an idea to help you receive healing in 30 days through the Word of God. For just 30 minutes for 30 days, you are challenged to study the Word of God (Bible) for 30 minutes for 30 days, as you believe for the healing you need, and sincerely do it. You will see your healing unfold. Make sure you whole-heartedly do it and do not do it grudgingly (2 Corinthians 9:7). When you grudgingly do something and do not have the heart, mind, and faith to do it, it will be ineffective. Make sure that you do not doubt at any time. Do your very best. If you mess up and get into the mode of doubting, quickly repent and ask God to forgive you and keep on going. <u>Please do not quit</u>. God will forgive you and meet you where you are. You will not lose your healing or your place with God. God loves when we are honest with ourselves, believing and trying.

It is encouraged that you do not read to see how many chapters you can read, but each day read for understanding and revelation knowledge and wisdom, and healing for what you need through His Word. God will speak to you about your current situation as you read, and He will open your eyes to a completely new way of thinking. Before you study, pray that God will reveal His Word especially for you and your need. Healing is always right at the door when you believe and do not doubt, all you have to do is open it. The Word of God (Bible) is the door.

The problem that many Christians have is the fact that they do not fully believe. While things are going right, they're on it—reading joyfully, speaking that they're healed, going and coming from church with fullness of worship and determination, working a 9 to 5 with their minds on good things, but right when their faith is challenged and tested, they quickly forget and give up. Do not allow satan to rob you of your miracle that God is waiting to give to you as you totally believe and do not doubt.

THINGS YOU NEED FOR THE 30 FOR 30
1. Faith
2. Bible *(Holy Bible or Study Bible) Best to use both for better understanding.*
3. Notebook tablet or note pad *(you may also use the one provided in this book).*
4. Pen or pencil
5. You may use your tablet, computer, cell phone, or iphone.

THINGS YOU WILL NEED TO DO FOR THE 30 FOR 30
1. Read the scripture(s) provided for you for that day (beginning with day 1).
2. You may get you a prayer partner(s) to agree with you and for your healing, if God leading. If you do not have a

prayer partner(s), they are not necessary for your healing. You can still receive your healing.
3. Answer the Power Questions.
4. Write the scriptures and notes in your book, tablet, notepad.
5. Pray the Power Prayer Changer at the end of each chapter.
6. Confess the Power Prayer Confession at the end of each chapter.
7. Believe each day for your healing and stay away from those who will make you doubt and give up.

REMOVE THE SPIRIT OF DISTRACTION

The spirit of distraction can keep you from your healing. Removing distraction can be one of the hardest things to do. However, when you make a conscious decision that nothing will stop you from getting what you need to be healed, the spirit of distraction will leave and you will do the initial things needed toward healing. This book requires interaction. It is best that you interact as you read. The 30 for 30 helps you do this through the reading of the scripture(s) each day, answering the Power Questions daily while praying the Power Prayer Changer prayer and confess the Power Prayer Confession. Also, writing scriptures and notes in your note pad or table; and verbally and prayerfully confess your healing over your life on a daily basis. This can all be done in the morning before starting your day, in your quiet time, during lunch, or even at night before bed. Whatever time you choose, please make sure you set aside a little more time than the 30 minutes so that you can have time for your confession and prayer. I have experienced that once you get into God's presence for 30 minutes, it usually turns into an hour or more. And, one thing I can say about getting in God's presence, is the more time I spent with Him, the quicker I heard from Him, and my healing instantly manifested. Please do not become discouraged if you can only spend 30 minutes per day, it does not mean that you will not receive His healing, because you can.

REMOVE THE SPIRIT OF PROCRASTINATION

You cannot win with the spirit of procrastination. Procrastination comes as a set-back. If you are in need of healing at this present moment, procrastination will kick it right out the door. It will postpone and delay what you need from God. In some cases, there may be a time when time is all you have. Do not allow satan to make you procrastinate on something you need. Get right to it, stick to it, and hang in there until you see your breakthrough. Amen? Amen.

RAISE YOUR EXPECTATIONS

Expect your healing from God. Do not just haphazardly read with no hope, no expectation of receiving your healing right away, reading and can't half remember what it is that you have read for that day, or allowing distractions from others (kids, husband or wife, family, friends, your favorite TV show, or unimportant phone calls). This is not raising your level of expectation, and you cannot expect God to do anything for you. You have to try your best to be consistent and have the power of expectation activated in your heart, mouth, mind, and soul. Your healing will come.

Most times your Word from God and/or your healing will come before your 30 days are up, and if that happens for you, great. I pray and believe with you that it will. If this happens for you, you are in encouraged to keep going until you get to the end of the 30 days so that you make sure you receive your healing to the fullest. As you receive your healing according to your faith and by the Word of God, and if it is before the 30 days, for the rest of the days it is also encouraged to give God the praise by thanking Him for your healing, power, strength, joy, love, peace, new mind, and whatever else you stand in need of. He will not hesitate to give it to you. Amen? Amen. Praise God.

> *Now unto him that is able to do exceeding abundantly above all that we ask or think, according to the power that worketh in us.*
> **Ephesians 3:20**

> *So shall my word be that goeth forth out of my mouth: it shall not return unto me void, but it shall accomplish that which I please, and it shall prosper in the thing whereto I sent it.*
> **Isaiah 55:11**

THE POWER QUESTIONS:

AS YOU READ AND STUDY EACH SCRIPTURE(S), ANSWER THE POWER QUESTIONS BELOW FOR ADDED DEVOTION EACH DAY: *(For additional space, you will need to write them down on your personal note pad, tablet, or other I requested that you get). If you do not have one, you may use the additional space below, and also on the 30 for 30 Note Pad for Study located at the end of this chapter.*

1. Explain what each scripture means to you.

2. How does this or these scripture(s) apply to your healing?

3. Do you see yourself healed through your daily devotion today? How and why?

Types of Sicknesses and Diseases are listed below, which one do you have?

- Accident (*unintentional injury*)
- Thyroid diseases
- Alzheimer's disease
- Amputation
- Arthritis
- Asperger syndrome
- Attention deficit hyperactivity disorder
- Autism
- Bipolar disorder
- Burn injury
- Cancer, *what type?* _____
- Celiac disease
- Cerebral palsy
- Charcot-Marie-Tooth disease
- Chronic fatigue syndrome
- Chronic obstructive pulmonary disease
- Crohn's disease
- Cystic fibrosis
- Dementia
- Depression
- Diabetes, *what type?* ___
- Dissociative disorder
- Down syndrome
- Dwarfism
- Eating disorders
- Epilepsy
- Fetal alcohol spectrum disorders
- Fibromyalgia
- Generalized anxiety disorder
- Hearing loss and deafness
- Heart disease
- HIV/AIDS
- Huntington's disease
- Intellectual disability
- Kidney disease
- Learning disabilities
- Lupus
- Multiple sclerosis
- Narcolepsy

- Obsessive-compulsive disorder
- Panic disorder
- Pervasive developmental disorders
- Polio and post-polio syndrome
- Post-traumatic stress disorder
- Psoriasis
- Rare diseases
- Easily distracted
- Schizophrenia
- Scleroderma
- Social phobia
- Speech and language disorders
- Spina bifida
- Spinal cord injury
- Stroke
- Thyroid diseases
- Traumatic brain injury
- Tuberous sclerosis
- Turner syndrome
- Ulcerative colitis
- Vision loss and blindness
- Williams syndrome
- *Gluttony (Excessive over eating)*
- *Laziness (Slothful)*
- *Don't Care*

If you see the sickness that is attacking you, write it here

_____
_____
_____
_____
_____

You should have written it down by now, if you have not because you do not see it, write it here _____

_____

Now that you have written it down, write the scripture(s) you are standing on during the 30 for 30 day healing challenge. You may use the ones I have provided for you on the next page, and also at the end of the book.

Please do not write a bunch of scriptures down that you know you are not going to stand on, and do not jot them down just because they are healing scriptures and do not pertain to your need. For example, healing scriptures that talk about healing the land or animals and not the human body. That is not what I am asking you to do. I am asking that you **ONLY** write the scripture(s) you are truly standing on that pertains only to you and your sickness. It may be only one, it may be several, or it just may be many. However, write them down in faith, believing and knowing that these scriptures are healing you through the power of Jesus Christ's Spirit.

Make sure you do not over-do it or try to be like someone else who may be stronger in faith than you are right now. Just do you and be who you are. God will meet you right where you are. He knows your weakness and He knows when you are trying and when you are not. He even knows when it is too hard for you to try to match up to someone else's faith that is stronger than you are right now. As you start where you are and keep on going, you too will be stronger just as they are.

If you know that you are not strong in this area of faith, then only start with one scripture and just confess that one scripture daily until it becomes embedded in your mind and spirit, and you know it by heart. You can also speak that scripture while you do other activities and go through your daily routine. Only if you believe, you should see immediate results. God is a miracle worker! I believe in you and I believe with you.

TEAM-UP!
Team up with a partner if you can find one for these 30 days and read together, pray together, and speak your Prayer Changer and Prayer Confession together. I have found that when you are in faith with more than one person, you are more encouraged to do it, believe it, complete it, and are stronger together to believe for

your healing(s). For example, it can be your spouse, or family member, child or children, sibling(s), coworker, pastor, church member, minister chosen, neighbor, or even just a friend. However, make sure whomever you choose to team up with, they have the same faith as you do to believe for your healing, and for themselves also, if theirs is needed. You do not want anybody who do not believe, is a negative person, jealous, do not like you, an unbeliever in God, do not want to see you healed, constantly gets mad at you, speaks against you, may not be negative toward your healing but is negative toward other things and people, inconsistent, brings distraction, makes you procrastinate, or never have time to read and believe with you.

If you have found you a partner or partners (you may have more than one), then get going right away, your healing awaits you. It's your time to be healed! It is your season! You have been waiting long enough, now your wait is over, so get going I believe in your healing and I believe in you….By the strips of Jesus Christ, **YOU ARE HEALED**! Amen! Praise GOD! Get Going…

30 for 30

Let's get started on your 30 for 30 day challenge! I'm excited and I know you are too. I believe miracles of healing are going to come for you through this 30 for 30 day challenge. I speak this and I believe this with you in the Name of Jesus!

LET'S BEGIN. Mark your start date, end date, and time below.
START DATE:_____ **START TIME:**_____
END DATE:_____ **END TIME:**_____
BEGIN ON THE NEXT PAGE...

Do the 30 Minute Study on Each Healing Scriptures Daily

Day 1	Psalm 107: 19-21, emphasis on verse 20
Day 2	Isaiah 53, emphasis on verse 4-5
Day 3	Psalm 30, emphasis on verse 2
Day 4	3 John 1:2
Day 5	1 Peter 2: 24
Day 6	Jeremiah 33: 6
Day 7	Psalm 41:3, Matt 11:28-30
Day 8	Matthew 8:1-17, emphasis on verses 16-17
Day 9	Matthew 6:4-13, emphasis on verse 6, 13
Day 10	Matthew 15:29-31
Day 11	Romans 4, emphasis on verses 16-21
Day 12	Romans 8:1, 11
Day 13	2 Corinthians 4:16-18
Day 14	Philippians 2:5, 13
Day 15	Philippians 4:6-9
Day 16	2 Timothy 1:7, Proverbs 3:5-6
Day 17	Matthew 18: 18-20
Day 18	Matthew 21:21-22
Day 19	Luke 6:17-19
Day 20	Ephesians 6:10-18
Day 21	Acts 3:1-9
Day 22	Acts 5:12-16
Day 23	Acts 10:38
Day 24	Hebrews 10:23, 35-39
Day 25	James 5:13-16
Day 26	1 John 3:21-22
Day 27	Jeremiah 17:14
Day 28	Jeremiah 30:17
Day 29	Psalm 103:3
Day 30	Exodus 15:26

30 for 30

Each day after you have completed your 30 minute scriptural study, read and verbally confess by faith the Power Prayer Changer below and the Prayer Changer Confession, daily on the next page.

Pray the Power Prayer Changer Below:

God, You have given me the keys to the Kingdom of Heaven, and I take authority against satan in every area of my life! I command him to leave right now! Matthew 18:18 says that You have given me the power to bind and to loose. Whatsoever I bind on earth, shall be bound in Heaven. And, whatsoever I loose on earth, shall be loosed in Heaven. I rebuke the sickness of _____

_____

_____

_____

by the Word of God, and I loose immediate healing by the power and precious Blood of Jesus Christ, and in the Name of the Lord Jesus Christ! Amen.

THE POWER PRAYER CHANGER DAILY <u>CONFESSION</u>

Pray the Prayer Changer Confession, Speak it By Faith:

Father I thank You that I can come before your presence with thanksgiving and enter into your courts with praise. I thank you that your Word in Scripture does not return back to you void according to Isaiah 55:11. I thank You that this *(write the sickness that is attacking you on the lines below)*

_____
_____
_____
_____
_____
_____

Does not live in my body any longer. I thank You that You were wounded for my transgressions, You were bruised for my iniquities, the chastisement of my peace was upon You, and with Your stripes I am healed. I claim my healing and victory today in Jesus Name! Amen.

30 for 30 Note Pad for Study

30 for 30 Note Pad for Study

5

Healing in the *Body*

Steps and Scripture to Ensure Healing

People all over the world are looking for the best CD, DVD, Christian TV show or ministerial segment, or even the latest bestselling book that will help them to be healed from their sicknesses. Unfortunately, the answer does not rest within an ordinary book, a human touch, or a verbal answer from man. It all comes from God above. Although He may use humans, a book, and he may even use a pastor, minsters, evangelists, or even global missionaries to lay hands and touch and agree or cast out the Spirit of sickness, the answer and healing still comes from God Himself. God does not need any substitutes. He is the God of healing all by Himself. The Word of God states in John 1:1,

> *"In the beginning was the Word, and the Word was with God, and the Word was God."*
> **John 1:1**

There is none like Him. The earth and everything on it was formed by Him. And as a result of this, we can be assured that no matter the illness that you are facing, great or small, hidden or seen, painful or content, God can heal you immediately. A perfect person to use was the woman who had an issue with blood. She knew that Jesus was healing and working miracles among the multitudes of people and she desperately figured, if she could just get to Jesus, she would be healed. Well, it worked, just as she made her way through the crowd to Jesus and touched the hem of His garment, she was immediately healed (Matthew 9:20-22).

> *(20) "And, behold, a woman, which was diseased with an issue of blood twelve years, came behind him, and touched the hem of his garment:*
> *(21) For she said within herself, if I may but touch his garment, I shall be whole.*
> *(22) But Jesus turned him about, and when he saw her, he said, Daughter, be of good comfort; thy faith hath made thee whole. And the woman was made whole from that hour."*
> **Matthew 9:20-22**

Healing in the Body

Now, this may sound very deep and could in no way possible be you running to a man you do not know, or a pastor or minister standing on a pulpit at a local church reaching his or her hand for you to come to the alter so they can pray for you and you immediately be healed. However, I can rest assure you that Christ comes in many different ways. You can never know who and how God chooses to heal you. So please do not limit God. He can do anything but fail and can use whom He so pleases to do it.

At this time in our lives we cannot afford to <u>NOT</u> believe. There is so much sickness in the land that it is impossible to sit and wobble in your sickness without calling on Jesus to help you. There is no time for the woe it's me syndrome. He is ready and willing and more than able to heal and to deliver you. When sickness is present, it attracts other spirits that come to make you even worse. This is why it is important to remain positive, watch what you say, and wait on the Lord until He comes.

When God moves, make sure you continuously cover yourself through prayer and constantly reading God's Word. For example, below are spirits that attach themselves to the spirit of diabetes. These sicknesses come to bring more upset if there is no faith and much negative speaking toward your sickness.

1. Gout
2. Fluid in the body
3. Fatigue

4. Excessive eating (heavy weight, eating disorders)
5. Easily Agitated
6. Coma

You are what you speak. You do not want to speak against your healing. The Word of God says:

> *"Keep thy tongue from evil, and thy lips from speaking guile."*
> **Psalms 34:13**

You must speak words of faith until your healing comes completely. The devil cannot hear your thoughts only God can, so when you speak against your healing and say words like, "I got diabetes and it ain't goin' away." Or, "There is no way God is going to heal this disease, it's much too great." Or, even this one, "I hate God for the sickness He gave me, all I do is sit in the hospital room all day long; and back and forth to the emergency room, I'll never be healed." Or, lastly, "This medicine is not going to help me get healed. Nope. Impossible. I guess it's my time to die now." These are just a few examples of what people speak as they do not realize that they are speaking against their healing. Your words become life, even when you are not sick. You cannot become frustrated and angry and allow the devil to make you speak (sin) things that you should not say, or speak against what the Word of God says about your healing. God can do anything but fail. You must make light of your situation even when you cannot physically see your full deliverance. You must speak that you are healed until it becomes a reality.

I can imagine the cripple man in Acts chapter 3, verses 1-10 who sat in front of the temple and begged for money. I believe he had faith and wanted to be healed due to the fact that he came to the temple everyday, and on that particular day it was early that afternoon right in time for the temple prayer service. He had much faith to believe that if he got to the temple to beg for money, he was going to get it. That was faith but not the faith that he needed. I also believe that somewhere on the inside of him there had to have been faith to want to be healed because I do not believe Jesus would have timed it just right for Peter and John to show up in front of the temple right when he was there with the detrimental need he had. Faith met faith. Belief met belief. God does not waste His time with unbelief or a doubting heart. He says *either be hot or cold, because if you're luke warm I will spew you out* (Revelation 3:15-16).

DO NOT SECOND GUESS GOD, especially when He gives you instructions. In Acts 10:9-17, God came to Peter in a vision and gave him specific instructions, but Peter based his opinion on what he saw instead of knowing, trusting, and relying on what God told Him to do. If God said so, that makes everything alright. It is the same thing with many Believers in Christ. God gives specific instructions and they tell God what is best or what they believe they need to do instead of saying in the beginning, "yes Lord, your Will not mine be done." Unfortunately, this happened three times with Peter. It took Peter three times to listen to what God had told him to do and to obey. Read and learn on the next page:

Healing in the Body

(9) "On the morrow, as they went on their journey, and drew nigh unto the city, Peter went up upon the housetop to pray about the sixth hour:

(10) And he became very hungry, and would have eaten: but while they made ready, he fell into a trance,

(11) And saw heaven opened, and a certain vessel descending unto him, as it had been a great sheet knit at the four corners, and let down to the earth:

(12) Wherein were all manner of fourfooted beasts of the earth, and wild beasts, and creeping things, and fowls of the air.

(13) And there came a voice to him, Rise, Peter; kill, and eat.

(14) But Peter said, Not so, Lord; for I have never eaten anything that is common or unclean.

*(15) And the voice spake unto him again the **second** time, What God hath cleansed, that call not thou common.*

*(16) This was done **thrice**: and the vessel was received up again into heaven.*

(17) Now while Peter <u>doubted in himself</u> what this vision which he had seen should mean, behold, the men which were sent from Cornelius had made enquiry for Simon's house, and stood before the gate,"

Acts 10:9-17

You must not doubt when God tells you to do something in regards to your need or with anything. There is always a reason behind it and the reason is for your good. Many times you can miss God and miss your season. You can also miss the great miracle that He has prepared for you if only you listen, receive, and obey at that moment.

The same thing happened to Elisha and the captain Naaman in 2 Kings 5:1-14. The captain was very sick with leprosy and heard about the prophet Elisha and his gift and faith to heal. He came to the prophet for help, and Elisha told him to go wash in the dirty Jordan seven times and he will be healed. The captain became angry and disagreed, and argued that there must be a better way to be healed. His servants talked to him, trying to convince him. The captain soon agreed and immediately after he jumped in the murky water, he was immediately and completely healed. Read and learn on the next page:

Healing in the Body

(1) "Now Naaman, captain of the host of the king of Syria, was a great man with his master, and honourable, because by him the LORD had given deliverance unto Syria: he was also a mighty man in valour, but he was a leper.

(2) And the Syrians had gone out by companies, and had brought away captive out of the land of Israel a little maid; and she waited on Naaman's wife.

(3) And she said unto her mistress, Would God my lord were with the prophet that is in Samaria! for he would recover him of his leprosy.

(4) And one went in, and told his lord, saying, Thus and thus said the maid that is of the land of Israel.

(5) And the king of Syria said, Go to, go, and I will send a letter unto the king of Israel. And he departed, and took with him ten talents of silver, and six thousand pieces of gold, and ten changes of raiment.

Stephanie Franklin

(6) And he brought the letter to the king of Israel, saying, Now when this letter is come unto thee, behold, I have $\boxed{\text{therewith}}$ sent Naaman my servant to thee, that thou mayest recover him of his leprosy.

(7) And it came to pass, when the king of Israel had read the letter, that he rent his clothes, and said, $\boxed{\text{Am}}$ I God, to kill and to make alive, that this man doth send unto me to recover a man of his leprosy? wherefore consider, I pray you, and see how he seeketh a quarrel against me.

(8) And it was $\boxed{\text{so}}$, when Elisha the man of God had heard that the king of Israel had rent his clothes, that he sent to the king, saying, Wherefore hast thou rent thy clothes? let him come now to me, and he shall know that there is a prophet in Israel.

(9) So Naaman came with his horses and with his chariot, and stood at the door of the house of Elisha.

(10) And Elisha sent a messenger unto him, saying, Go and wash in Jordan seven times, and thy flesh shall come again to thee, and thou shalt be clean.

> *(11) But Naaman was wroth, and went away, and said, Behold, I thought, He will surely come out to me, and stand, and call on the name of the LORD his God, and strike his hand over the place, and recover the leper.*
>
> *(12) Are not Abana and Pharpar, rivers of Damascus, better than all the waters of Israel? may I not wash in them, and be clean? So he turned and went away in a rage.*
>
> *(13) And his servants came near, and spake unto him, and said, My father, if the prophet had bid thee do some great thing, wouldest thou not have done it? how much rather then, when he saith to thee, Wash, and be clean?*
>
> *(14) Then went he down, and dipped himself seven times in Jordan, according to the saying of the man of God: and his flesh came again like unto the flesh of a little child, and he was clean.*
>
> **2 Kings 5:1-14**

After reading these passages of scripture, you see how Peter and the Captain Naaman second-guessed and doubted within themselves what God told them to do because they went by what it looked like and not by what God said? You must trust God enough to know that He is I Am and the pure fact that He made Heaven and earth, and He knows all things. Never second guess God, or think you know better than God, or you know what's best for you than God does. He created you and He knows you better than you know yourself. His thoughts are not your thoughts, His ways are not your ways (Isaiah 55:8). He does not think like us. We are only humans that can be here one minute and gone at any given moment. But God will last forever. Do not ask questions, just say, *"yes Lord, I will obey. Yes Lord, I will trust You. Yes Lord, I will not go by what my current situation looks like right before me, but I will choose to go by what You have told me to do, as I have put my trust in You."*

You do not have the power to know more than God. If you did, you would be Him and certainly would not need Him. Make today your day to trust Him in how He wants to heal you and the process that He is taking you through to get to it. You can rest assure that He will not fail you. It will be rewarding and you will not regret it. Amen? Praise God.

I will share an awesome testimony of how God healed a woman who had stage four cancer. She told me that she had stage four cancer and I prayed and agreed with her for her healing. When she went back for her check-up, the doctor stated that she no longer had cancer in her body. The key here is, she first had faith. Then I had faith for and with her as I prayed for her and with her. As she confessed the Word of God daily as she and I agreed before returning to the doctor's office, as a result, she received notice by the doctor that she was healed. She did not wait until she got to the doctor to hear him say that she was healed, she had faith and already knew that God had healed her because she trusted God and had faith to know that He is faithful and His Word cannot lie (Numbers 23:19-20). Her **confirmation** came when she heard the words of the doctor. But, the real Doctor in Heaven had already let her know that she was healed before that day. You have to believe that same way. I believe that you can do it. Just relax, take one day at a time as God will meet you where you are, and believe you are healed and you are. You can do it.

> *(19) "God is not a man, that he should lie; neither the son of man, that he should repent: hath he said, and shall he not do it? or hath he spoken, and shall he not make it good?"*
>
> *(20) "Behold, I have received commandment to bless: and he hath blessed; and I cannot reverse it."*
>
> **Numbers 23:19-20**

In order to experience true immediate healing, you must match your faith with God's faith to be healed. For example, in Acts 14:1-18, during Paul's great ministry as he preached in Lystra, he experienced a cripple man needing to be healed. It was obvious that he could not walk by the fact that he could not stand up and walk. Here is the key to my example, verses 9-10, *"He (the cripple man) was listening to Paul as he talked, and Paul, gazing intently at him (the cripple man) and observing **that he had faith to be healed**. Paul shouted at him saying, stand erect on your feet! And he leaped up and walked."* I say this to say, that healing will not come if you are making the preacher, pastor, minister, leader, whom ever is praying healing with you and for you come if you do not have faith to believe you <u>can</u> be healed <u>first</u>. The connection happens when faith happens, and if there is two agreeing together, then they two must believe. Many times people wait on others to do all of the work and then get upset when they do not experience healing or experience it right away. It is according to <u>your</u> faith. The cripple man had faith to believe that he could be healed. In fact, I believe that he saw himself healed first. Paul shouted into the crowd at him and first discerned that he had faith, which was the connection for him to be healed, and then physically brought the manifestation of his faith alive by telling him to stand up and walk. So, he did, by his faith. I know this sounds repetitive, but it is true. All healing is, is the act of faith. This is an action word. It takes faith to move God, without it, you cannot please God (Hebrews 11:6). This has to work for all of God's people. I will give you a testimony on you first having faith to believe that you are healed, and then with the other person agreeing with you and praying for and with you, immediate healing will come forth. It does not always have to be a great detrimental need of healing, it can be something much more minor. However, I believe all sickness, whether minor or great should always be treated the same. Here is the testimony. There was a woman who had a terrible flu. She had a terrible flu and a very high fever and needed someone to pray for her. She called and asked me to come over to her house and pray for her. When I arrived, she was laying in her bed of affliction, and as I laid my hand on her head and began to pray against the sickness of infirmity, she immediately felt better as the fever left. Her sickness immediately left because she believed that she was healed. As I prayed for her, I knew that she believed because I could feel the sickness leave her body. She believed. I believed. We believed together and the sickness of infirmity could not remain in her body, so it left. This is what I mean when I say healing cannot come if you do not believe for yourself. You cannot wait on others to believe for you in order to receive healing, you must first believe. When you first believe, healing will come immediately as hers did.

You may ask why did she need me to come and pray for her if she already believed? I will answer, at times we believe, but need someone with more faith because at the time she was too weak to do it alone. Although her healing was coming, it came faster with two or more agreeing (Matthew 18:19).

Do Not Become Discouraged

Do not become discouraged or intimidated when you see others healed right away and you do not. It does not mean that you do not believe, it may mean that you need to increase your faith a little bit more. Find out what you may be doing to hinder or prolong your healing. It could be something very small. The Bible only requires that you have mustard seed faith (Matthew 17:20). Have you ever seen a mustard seed before? It is a tiny seed that can easily get lost in your hand. This is the amount of faith that Jesus requires from us to be healed. You may say, "I believe that God can heal me but I do not see results." Well, I will help you by responding that you must imagine that your sickness is gone everyday until you feel, see, and know that what you imagined is no longer inside of your body. You must imagine that your migraine headaches are gone. You must imagine that your bodily pain and stiffness is gone. You must imagine that your flu symptoms are gone. You must imagine that your blood pressure will not rise anymore. You must imagine that your diabetes is no longer there. You must imagine that the cancer is no longer in your body. You must imagine that you can visually see. You must imagine that you have a new heart or a new kidney, and so forth. Whatever illness you may be encountering, imagine that it is gone, stand on the Word of God, plead the Blood of Jesus, and stand on your healing scriptures of faith and healing that I have provided for you in this book. You may also use other scriptures you may have. There must be a connection.

So, here is an example of the connection:

HAVE FAITH & BELIEVE *(believe by imagining that your sickness is gone and no longer there)*

+ CONFESS *(verbally speak as you read the healing and faith scriptures from the Word of God over your life <u>that you are healed</u> and not in need of healing on a daily basis)*

= MANIFESTED HEALING

From the Word of God's Perspective:

The cripple man **had faith first** before Peter asked him if he wanted to be healed (Acts 3:5).

+ **CONFESSION and prayer was made** by Peter and the cripple man agreeing. *(Can also be done by your faith alone.)*

= HEALING came forth immediately.

6

Healing in Your Praise

The Praise Break

I **don't know if you realize it or not,** but there is power in your praise. You do not realize how much power you have until you are depressed and begin to sing songs of praise. Something supernatural, spiritual, and miraculous happens and you suddenly realize that you are no longer depressed. There is a shift in the atmosphere, because you are the atmosphere. You change the atmosphere by <u>your</u> praise. You are responsible for your praise. No one can praise God for you but you. No one can praise God out of his or her situation like you can. Many

Christians do not realize that when you praise God, everything that is not like God sheds off and immediately you are set free.

There have been times when I was in the mist of praise and worship with other Saints of God during a church service. At first, the praise and worship service had just begun with clapping our hands. If you were to look around the congregation, you could tell some were truly trying to praise and worship God, while others were not quite so into it yet. However, when the worship leader began to shout into the mic as to get everyone more involved, the Spirit of the Lord came in and the atmosphere began to change. You could literally feel an immediate shifting in the atmosphere. Everything that I was going through was no longer on my mind. The Spirit of Depression immediately left from me and I felt light enough to dance in the Spirit. With that said, when you make a conscious decision to praise God no matter what your circumstances are, and no matter what sickness is attacking you at the time, praise God on purpose and trust me, it or they will immediately fall off of you. The key here is, you must praise and worship God in Spirit and in truth (John 4:24).

> *"God is a Spirit: and they that worship him must worship him in spirit and in truth."*
>
> **John 4:24**

SHARE YOUR TESTIMONY IF THIS HAS HAPPENED TO YOU

_____

_____

_____

_____

_____

_____

_____

God is serious about giving you what you need. He is ready to bless you and as you praise Him whether in your car, at home during your quiet time, or during worship service at church, do it with your whole heart, mind, Spirit and soul and you will experience a shifting from within. Sickness, spiritual chains, depression, oppression, stress, anxiety, fear, hatred, anger, and worry, will be removed immediately. I encourage you to cry out to God with a nothing else matter cry, shout, and attitude. I believe God used worship for a place just for His people and Him to experience alone, as well as corporately. The power of praise and worship is seen in the Old Testament with Miriam and all of the women worshipping the Lord our God. Look on the next page.

> *(20) "And Miriam the prophetess, the sister of Aaron, took a timbrel in her hand; and all the women went out after her with timbrels and with <u>dances</u>."*
>
> *(21) "And Miriam answered them, Sing ye to the LORD, for he hath triumphed gloriously; the horse and his rider hath he thrown into the sea."*
>
> **Exodus 15:20-21**

Worship was created in the Old Testament with Moses and the Israelite's celebration over the victory of crossing the Red Sea. Miriam and the women went out and began to PRAISE and to WORSHIP God by singing songs as they used instruments and dancing. In other words, they partied in the Lord. They got their groove on for the Lord. They gave God their best praise because of what He had done for them. God is faithful and just as He saved them, He can save and heal you too through your true praise and worship. Just try it as you trust Him and praise Him. He's ready to give you total victory in Jesus Name.

If your praise has been challenged and you have given up on God, be encourage to know that God is a God of another chance and He is ready to pour out the ministry of reconciliation when you come back to Him. It will be as if you never left Him. He understands your position and how you feel, and He is ready to heal you and bring you to a place of peace in Him. You may ask, "how do I come back to God?" I will answer, by repenting (telling Him you are sorry) and by acknowledging that you love and need Him. As you lift up your hands and close your eyes in true worship as a sign to surrender, He will come in and do just what you are asking of Him. He is sovereign and full of mercy and grace, for it is sufficient.

Experience His peace and comfort today as you worship Him in Spirit and in truth.

7

Power to Maintain Your

Healing

Remind God of His Word Daily

By the strips of Jesus Christ, you <u>were</u> healed. (1 Peter 2:24).

Maintaining your healing comes with trusting in God's Word daily to keep His promise of healing that He gave to you whether your healing came a second ago, or fifty years ago. It is a daily trust, not by asking Him did He heal you, it is a daily trust of faith by speaking your confession that you are healed. Look on the next page.

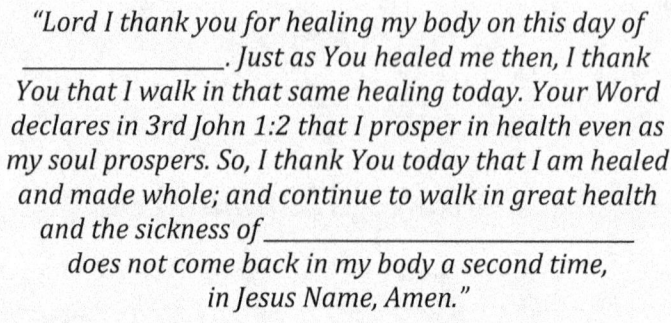

"Lord I thank you for healing my body on this day of _____. Just as You healed me then, I thank You that I walk in that same healing today. Your Word declares in 3rd John 1:2 that I prosper in health even as my soul prospers. So, I thank You today that I am healed and made whole; and continue to walk in great health and the sickness of_____ does not come back in my body a second time, in Jesus Name, Amen."

That is how you maintain your healing. It is in what you believe. It is in what you speak. If you believe that you are still sick, then you will struggle and be sick. If you believe and <u>speak</u> that you are still sick, then you will struggle and be sick. However, if you believe and speak that you are healed, then you will be healed and walk victoriously in good health.

Watching what you speak is another means of maintaining your healing. The Word of God states that death and life is in the power of the tongue (Proverbs 18:21). So, watch what you speak at all times and be slow to speak and quick to listen (James 1:19). I realize this may be a struggle for some, especially those who love to talk and struggle with gossip. It is a day-to-day walk, and a day-to-day trust in God for everything. Not only for healing but also for peace of mind, to love no matter what, to stir up your joy in every situation—good or bad; and even those areas where you may be troubled and discouraged. It is a constant battle for some but you can do it. You can win. You are victorious in Jesus Name!

Abide in God's presence and spend time with Him. Try my 30 for 30 healing challenge for 30 minutes for 30 days in chapter four. I pray that it will bless and change your life forever and the days that will follow. I pray that you will follow the 30 for 30, even after your month is done, and allow it to become a way of life for you. For just 30 minutes a day, spend time with God and thank Him for your healing and great health and peace of mind. Spend time reading and saturating yourself in the scriptures. God will not hesitate to give you what you need. It worked for me during the downiest times of my life so I know it will work for you. Remember, it is in what you believe. **YOU MUST BELIEVE AND YOU MUST KEEP YOUR FAITH** in order for your healing to manifest and for it to remain.

CONCLUSION

It is my utmost desire that God's people walk in the fullness of great health and blessing as they live a life of total victory over the power of sickness.

"The Power of Healing" has come as a Biblical guide to help the Believer to stand on the Word of God (Bible) for total healing. Everything you need is found in the Word of God. There are some people who look to other sources for potential healing, but I encourage you to look to God through His Word, through prayer, and through your daily power faith confession as you speak over your life that you are healed in Jesus Name on a daily basis. I believe with you, and believe that you are healed by the Blood of Jesus Christ, and by the Word of God that promises to heal and make you whole (Acts 9:34).

Aeneas was paralyzed and in his bed of affliction for eight years when God used Peter and miraculously healed and made him whole (Acts 9:32-34). He walked immediately. He could have given up and said "forget it, God can't heal. I'll just die on my bed of affliction." But God said different. Just because you may not see or experience your healing right away, does not mean that God is not mindful of you and He has forgotten about you. He is on the

Conclusion

way. Just keep the faith and never give up. You never know when God is going to visit you just as He did Aeneas.

INDEX

INDEX/SOURCES:

1. http://www.diabetes.org/diabetes-basics/myths/

BIBLICAL INDEX SOURCES FROM EACH CHAPTER

INTRODUCTION
- *Matthew 17: 20*
- *Ephesians 1:19*
- *Ephesians 3:20*

CHAPTER 1
- *Luke 12:12*
- *Matthew 15:18*
- *Proverbs 3:5-6*
- *Galatians 6:9*
- *Ephesians 3:20*
- *Deuteronomy 31:8*
- *Romans 8:37*
- *Jeremiah 29:11*

CHAPTER 2
- *Philippians 2:5*
- *Isaiah 53:5*
- *Acts 4: 24-31*
- *John 14:18, 8-18*
- *Acts 4:32*
- *Matthew 18:16*
- *Philippians 4:11*

CHAPTER 3
- *Acts 3:1-10*
- *Revelations 3:15-16*

CHAPTER 4
- *2 Corinthians 9:7*
- *Ephesians 3:20*
- *Isaiah 53:5*
- *3 John 2*
- *Exodus 15:26*
- *Matthew 18:18*
- *Isaiah 55:11*

CHAPTER 5
- *John 1:1*
- *Matthew 9:20-22*
- *Psalms 34:13*
- *Acts 3:1-10*
- *Revelations 3:15-16*
- *Acts 10:9-17*
- *Matthew 18:19*
- *2 Kings 5:1-14*
- *Numbers 23:19-20*
- *Acts 14:1-18*
- *Hebrews 11:6*
- *Acts 3:5*
- *Matthew 17:20*
- *Isaiah 55:8*

CHAPTER 6
- *John 4:24*
- *Exodus 15:20-21*

CHAPTER 7
- *Proverbs 18:21*
- *James 1:19*

ADDITIONAL HEALING SCRIPTURES FOR YOUR STUDY:

Exodus 15:26
Exodus 23:25-26
Ezra 2:65
Deuteronomy 7:14-15
Deuteronomy 30:19-20
I Kings 8:56
Psalm 103:1-5
Psalm 107:17, 19-21
Psalm 118:17
Psalm 41:3
Psalm 41:1
Psalm 30:2
Proverbs 4:20-24
Isaiah 41:10
Isaiah 53:4-5
Jeremiah 1:12
Jeremiah 17:14
Jeremiah 30:17
Jeremiah 33:6
Joel 3:10
James 5:16
Nahum 1:9
Matthew 1:34
Matthew 8:2-3
Matthew 8:16-17
Matthew 11:28-30
Matthew 15:29-31
Matthew 18:18-20
Matthew 19:26
Matthew 21:21-22
Mark 6:13
Mark 9:23
Mark 10:27
Mark 11:22-24
Mark 16:14-18
Luke 6:17-19
Luke 9:2
Luke 13:16
Acts 5:12-16
Acts 10:38
Acts 28:9
Romans 4:16-21
Romans 8:1, 11
2 Corinthians 4:16-18
2 Corinthians 10:3-5
2 Corinthians 5:18
2 Corinthians 30:20
Galatians 3:13-14, 29
Ephesians 6:10-17
Philippians 2:5, 13
Philippians 4:6-9
2 Timothy 1:7
Hebrews 10:23
Hebrews 10:35-39
Hebrews 11:11
Hebrews 13:8
Hebrews 12:12-13
James 4:7
James 5:13-16
1 Peter 2:24
1 John 3:19-20
1 John 3:21-22
1 John 5:4
1 John 5:14-15
3 John 1:2
Revelation 12:11

Note Pad as You Study

Additional Note Pad as You Study

Stephanie Franklin

Additional Note Pad as You Study

Stephanie Franklin

Additional Note Pad as You Study

Stephanie Franklin

Additional Note Pad as You Study

Stephanie Franklin

Additional Note Pad as You Study

Stephanie Franklin

Additional Note Pad as You Study

OTHER BOOKS BY STEPHANIE

FICTION NOVELS & MOTIVATIONAL BOOKS:

1. When Ramona Got Her Groove Back from God
2. My Song of Solomon
3. My Song of Solomon *Prayer Journal*
4. God Loves Thugs Too!
5. The Locker Room Experience: *For the Struggling Athlete & Coach, & Tips on How to Get Recruited in Sports*
6. REshape YOU: *A Fitness Guide to Teach You How to Create the NEW YOU from the Inside Out*
7. REshape YOU Elderly Fitness Exercises & Eating Plan Book: *A Fitness Book of Simple Exercises & Eating Plans for the Elderly*

MINISTRY BOOKS & WORKBOOK:

8. Position Your Faith for Great Success
9. Position Your Faith for Great Success *Workbook*
10. The Purpose Chaser: *For Children Ages 5 to 12*
11. Church Hurt: *How to Heal & Overcome It*
12. *The Power of Healing*
13. *The Power of the Holy Spirit*

To Reorder Books or request book signings, speaking engagements, and/or workshops and/or seminars, email or visit Website(s):

Stephanie Franklin
info@stephaniefranklinministries.org
www.stephaniefranklin.org
www.stephaniefranklinministries.org
www.heavenlyrealmpublishing.com
1-866-216-0696, EXT. 1

Stephanie Franklin

Stephanie Franklin Ministries
PO Box 682532
Houston, TX 77268

Join Today!

Become A Purpose Chaser!

When you join the Purpose Chasers, you are saying that, "I'm going to chase after my purpose and dreams no matter what. I am going to chase after God with all I have no matter what anybody says. I'm going to chase with a good attitude, I am going to chase in my home, in my community, in my school, in my church; all over the world!"

JOIN TODAY! VISIT:
www.stephaniefranklin.org

YOU MAY ALSO EMAIL ME TODAY!
info@stephaniefranklinministries.org

Order Your, "I'm A Purpose Chaser" T-Shirt today!

VISIT MY WEBSITE TO ORDER:
www.stephaniefranklin.org

Send email for accurate size and price:
info@stephaniefranklinministries.org

or you may visit: All Christian Bookstores, Barnes & Noble, Amazon.com, Borders, Books-A-Million, and any Bookstore near you.

Meet the Author

Stephanie Franklin, M.A. (T.S.)

Obtains a Master of Arts degree in Theological Studies and has a vision to reach the world with her mentoring, teaching, life coaching, and preaching ministry. She has a heart to reach the youth and young adults along with the entire family, bringing them all together as a unified fold. One of her greatest desires is to be used by God in whatever capacity He chooses.

www.ingramcontent.com/pod-product-compliance
Lightning Source LLC
LaVergne TN
LVHW051846080426
835512LV00018B/3104